Already Beautiful

Written and illustrated by
Kelly M. Harkcom

©2021 by Kelly M. Harkcom

All rights reserved. No part of this publication may be reproduced or transmitted in any form or by any means, electronic or mechanical, including photocopying, recording, or any other information storage and retrieval system, without the written permission of the publisher.

Internet addresses given in this book were accurate at the time it went to press.

Printed in the United States of America

Published in Hellertown, PA

Library of Congress Control Number 2021917747

ISBN 978-1-952481-57-4

2 4 6 8 10 9 7 5 3 1

For more information or to place bulk orders, contact the publisher at Jennifer@BrightCommunications.net.

To my family, Sean, Rylan, and Sydney,
thank you for being my support system in
my health, wealth, and happiness.

To my mom and dad,
thank you for never letting me say "I can't,"
and always encouraging me to try something new.

To my students, past, present, and future,
thank you for being my inspiration in my job
as your teacher and in my writing as an author.

To Pam, my source of encouragement,
my sounding board, and my friend.

Every morning, Brianna secretly watched her mom put on makeup.

She loved colors and the way they looked on her mom, like a rainbow painted across her face.

"My mom is beautiful," she whispered to herself.

Her teacher wore makeup, too,
though not quite as much,
and was **also beautiful,**
so Brianna thought she wanted
to be just as beautiful as them.

Before bedtime, Brianna
tiptoed into her mom's room
and borrowed some of her
eyeshadow and lipstick
to wear to school the next day.

The next morning, Brianna strutted confidently through the classroom door, showing off her **new colorful face.**

Mrs. Howard noticed Brianna's sudden change in appearance and said, "Brianna, I'm so happy you're here today! I have a project I know you're going to love."

Mrs. Howard asked the class
to make a list of things that are
made beautiful by nature.

Mia raised her hand and excitedly said,
"Sunsets! Sunsets are beautiful!"

Mrs. Howard added "sunsets" to the list.

Zachary blurted out,
"Birds are pretty amazing
the way they soar across the sky, and
they have beautiful colors."

Another great suggestion
was added to the list.

Rainbows,

flowers,

and **a new snowfall**
were also added to
the growing list.

Ii Jj Kk Ll Mm Nn

What is beautiful?
- sunsets
- birds
- rainbow
- flowers
- snow falli[ng]

Mrs. Howard then asked the class to select one of the options on the list or to choose their own idea for their next writing assignment, a poem about something **naturally beautiful.**

Brianna simply could not decide.

The next day, Mrs. Howard greeted the students at the door looking a bit…different.

Different but still beautiful.

Brianna could not figure out what was different, and she kept staring at her teacher all day.

When it was time for writing,
Mrs. Howard asked the class if they had
decided what beautiful thing they were
going to be writing about.

Everyone nodded "Yes,"
and Brianna's eyes suddenly lit up.

She finally figured out what was different about Mrs. Howard!

Mrs. Howard wasn't wearing makeup, but she was **still beautiful!**

Suddenly, Brianna knew just the right topic for her poem.

Brianna got home that day
to find her mom in her bedroom
taking off her makeup.

Her mom didn't need to wear it either.
She was already beautiful.

Brianna still loved makeup
and wore it often…

…down the runway
of the living room floor.

Everyone is beautiful inside and out It's not about your style It's your heart that really counts.

About the Creator

Kelly Harkcom developed a love of books before she could even talk. She has been a kindergarten teacher for many years and enjoys collecting far too many picture books to read to her young students and to her own two children. She loves everything about the writing and illustrating process and hopes to show other aspiring writers, young and old, that your dream of writing a book is attainable!

When Kelly is not creating, she enjoys spending time outdoors with her family. She loves animals, visiting the beach, and a good cup of coffee. She resides in Eastern Pennsylvania with her husband and two children.

CPSIA information can be obtained
at www.ICGtesting.com
Printed in the USA
BVHW061620041121
620781BV00018B/604